HOW TO ENGAGE, INSPIRE AND STIMULATE YOUR AUDIENCE

Dan Terry

Enjoy

Dan

How to ENGAGE, INSPIRE and STIMULATE your AUDIENCE

Copyright © 2009 by Dan Terry

ISBN 978-0-9563723-0-7

For Tracey, Ruth and Katie.

Contents

Acknowledgements

WOULD LIKE TO thank my wife Tracey, and my daughters Ruth and Katie, for their patience and loving support, without which this book would not have been possible.

Special thanks are also due to Harry J. Brice for his advice, encouragement, and patience during the endless re-drafts, phone calls and requests to change just one more bit.

Thank you to Shelley-Dee Kirkbride for the wonderful illustrations (shelleydee23@hotmail.co.uk).

Thanks also to Paul Malatratt and Steve Golembiewski for your valuable time and advice, to Darren Ford, Andrew Gordon, Vicki Yates, Maggie Lucas, Mark McKenny, Nigel Richardson, Kieron Shanks, Kate Shaw, David Day and John McKay, you've all been terrific. And, of course, all of the delegates over the years for the inspiration, and my many friends and family for their faith and endless support.

Preface

FIRST MET Dan Terry over five years ago at a seminar in London. Since then we have become colleagues, friends and co-presenters on numerous occasions. It is a privilege for me to write a few words as the foreword to this book. I have seen firsthand Dan captivating an audience and I have often thought "*Wow, how does he do that?*" I must confess that I have also thought "*I wish I could do that.*" By carefully observing what he does, I have improved my skills as a presenter, without ever attempting to become a copy or clone of the original. This book will help anyone who has to speak in public. It will be of use to people who have to speak as part of their working life , trainers, presenters and teachers, or those who just speak occasionally at weddings or parties.

There is an old adage in the world of training that some people will get it from just being told, others will need to see it, and still others will need to experience it. Reading this book will tell you what Dan does in order to be a truly captivating public speaker. If you are able to attend one of Dan's speaking engagements then you will be able to observe him firsthand. In order to have the experience of what it is like to captivate an audience you will need to try out the things Dan writes about in this book. And as Dan would say, remember the three **A**'s – when you do something for the first time it's **A**wkward, but if you keep **A**pplying it, it becomes **A**utomatic.

Keith Aiton, EAF International
Master NLP Coach and Trainer

Introduction

"You don't have to be great to start but you have to start to be great"

Zig Ziglar

THIS BOOK WON'T tell you how to write a presentation or put together a course. It won't tell you what kind of things you should and shouldn't include, and it won't help you design leaflets or course notes. Writing a presentation, talk, seminar or course is covered in other books. This book WILL tell you, once you've written your presentation or course, how to engage with the audience and have them on the edge of their seats, hanging on to every word you say.

Imagine facilitating a course where you can really feel the energy in the room, and you are delivering fantastic results, time and time again. This is what this book will help you to achieve through training and presenting.

Nowadays trainers, facilitators, presenters and sales people have to be at the top of their game, as new technology and transport shrinks the world, whilst the world itself becomes increasingly competitive. You only have to look towards China and see the strides they have made recently. The same principle applies in the training field, and companies that traditionally have employed and developed their own in-house experts and trainers can now afford to shop around, sometimes worldwide, for external people.

Out sourcing has become very common especially in the field of training and personnel development, so get prepared to beat the competition.

I've spent the last decade training thousands of company employees and during this time I've become very frustrated hearing about the problems my clients have had with their previous training providers.

So I decided to do some research into the phenomenon, to try and develop an understanding of what constituted a really good and interesting course. At the time I was working primarily in the field of Health and Safety, which (lets be brutally honest) isn't the most invigorating or exciting of topics. If I could understand the essential elements of presenting this topic in an engaging and entertaining way, then any other topic could be brought alive regardless of how dry and dusty the subject matter might initially seem.

The fields of training and personal development offer fantastic opportunities to touch people's lives in profound ways. At the very least, we owe it to the many thousands of people who attend the many thousands of courses that run each year, in thousands of organisations all over the country and overseas, to offer our courses and presentations to them in such a way that they remember what they've been taught, can act upon this new knowledge immediately, and have a good time doing it.

I've written this book in 10 simple steps, breaking down each of the techniques so that your audience can be quickly and irreversibly hooked. This book will, I sincerely hope, intrigue and inspire you, even if you apply only one of the steps. Every chapter is full of ideas and techniques that I have used to train staff in many organisations both in the UK and overseas and they've been tried and tested over many years. Your challenge is to take on at least one a month (or for a greater challenge, one a week) and apply it. Your career and those of your delegates will take on a whole new meaning.

Learn to master the whole group, even the show offs, or the ones who don't particularly want to be there. This book can be used as a workbook – open it at any chapter and apply the techniques almost immediately.

A number of years ago I heard of a delegate who, after attending a four day course (not one of mine I hasten to add), went back to work and almost immediately fell into scalding water (metaphorically speaking). Apparently it wasn't a case of (a) "it-won't-happen-to-me" attitude, or (b) complacency or negligence. It was simply the case that the course was so dull that most of the messages and training had literally "gone out of the window".

This book explains how to make a presentation memorable and without knowing it the people/delegates on your course start to do the things you discussed and continue to do them long after the course has finished. How good would that be?

I set about modelling how the best presenters delivered their material and how they interacted, engaged and energised the group. The one thing that all the best presenters did was start with the delegate in mind, rather than the topic being taught. If your presentation methods and style are delegate focussed, you can gain fantastic results. And you can do this before you even start your presentation!

Above all have fun

Chapter 1

The Rules have changed

CAN YOU REMEMBER the name of your favourite teacher when you were at school? What subject did they teach? Did you do well in that particular subject?

Now, can you remember the dullest and most boring teacher(s) at school? Most people can remember the name of their favourite teacher and the subject they taught, and it's usually true that when a child engages fully with a teacher their understanding and performance within the subject improves. So, it's not surprising that (after all these years) you can still remember your favourite teacher, yet generally people find the names of dull or boring teachers more difficult to recall.

Now, thinking back, can you remember the first in-house company training course you had to attend? Did the instructor put you to sleep with the overhead transparencies or a PowerPoint presentation, but you were still expected to remember all the information and fill in an assessment form afterwards? What was that like?

Conversely, have you ever been on a course that inspired you, so much so that you took it further and applied what you learned?

These two examples help to show how we rarely remember

things that bore us and don't stimulate us. If training does not invigorate both our imagination and creative thinking, as well as our professional or personal knowledge, it becomes a total waste of time, effort, and money.

In the past, the general approach was for lecturers to lecture, and the audience to just shut up and listen. It has taken many generations for teachers to discover that people do not learn effectively in that way, and they never did. So, the rules have had to change. The age of instructors' with sergeant major's swagger canes, regularly beating the desk or podium to ensure attention is (I hope) long gone.

But the effects of this approach isn't, and it's a great shame because many thousands of people still sit through many hours of courses, and ultimately all that the lecturers and trainers achieve is to bore the pants off the delegates.

I remember attending one particular works seminar because I fell sound asleep on the front row, right under the lecturer's nose! Around sixty of us were attending that course and many of us had been out the night before for a few beers. Now, I know that this wasn't perhaps the best way to prepare for a course, but there we are - that was what happened.

The trainers' voice droned on monotonously, which was just about the best alternative sleeping pill anyone could have. It was such a shame because with a little thought and planning the subject could have been a really interesting one. However, it wasn't to be.

Within minutes I had slipped blissfully away to dreamland, and within what must have been a few minutes I suddenly heard a voice bellowing – "AM I BORING YOU?" With this I sat up straight, slightly confused, apologised and managed somehow to remain conscious for the rest of the session. After the break I sat in a different place, near the back of the room, and to my pleasant astonishment there were many others dropping off to sleep as well. The day dragged on, and I'm sorry to say I can't even remember what subjects were covered. I was eternally grateful when the course was concluded.

Do you know what was so sad? The instructor was completely unaware of the level of boredom that he was inflicting on us! And despite the obvious problems associated with this approach, there are still some trainers out there who still use the old rules. You probably know one or two?

Having seen and lived through the "bad old days", it is time for us to consider how the "Good New Days" need to be shaped. But first, there are two little phrases that must be learned by heart.

- The trainer does not know everything.
- The only difference between the trainer and the delegate is that the trainer has been a delegate longer.

Old rules	New rules
• Lecture to the delegates • Stick to rigid syllabus • Read off the slide show • Overload with information • Written closed book test • Controlling	• Get to know the delegates preferred learning style • Deliver flexibility • Have group interaction and engagement • Use humour, fun to create interest, and feedback • Nurture

Let's disregard the old rules, and look at these new rules in more detail.

New Rules Get to know the delegates' preferred learning style

M ANY TRAINERS/SPEAKERS have one preferred way of delivering their information. Practice makes perfect, and after a time they find what works for them and fall into their comfort zone in terms of presentation style. But, in many cases it doesn't occur to them, that delegates have many different ways of learning and understanding in terms of course delivery, and may require a variety of ways to keep them interested.

Trainers/speakers must be sensitive and sympathetic to the reactions and interactions of their delegates, and need to have flexibility in their methods of delivery. Preparation is the key to enable this to happen.

Similarities can be drawn with respect to stand-up comedians. They have to be thoroughly prepared, better than any other performer, to deliver a fixed script so that all the right jokes are delivered at the right time and in the right order. Also, vary it according to the reactions of their audience to keep the flow of information at the optimum level, and have an armoury of quips and put downs that can be immediately used to stop a heckler in their tracks and bring the show back on course. As a result they deliver a relaxed and seemingly informal presentation of their material, based on many hours solid preparation and practice time.

The various learning styles are dealt with later in this book, and being able to deliver the essential elements of any course or presentation in line with each learning style will enable you to choose the right approach with the audience when the crucial time comes.

1 Deliver Flexibility

Some topics have to be more rigid in terms of the data being conveyed than others; for example Health and Safety law, employment law, tax law, etc., are based on solid facts and rules, rigidly laid down with no interpretation required at all. So the general assumption is that these dry and inflexible subjects have to be presented in a dry and inflexible way. This is not the case at all. The only difference between these and so called "lighter" topics, like sales skills, killer marketing techniques, Neuro Linguistic Programming (NLP) training, etc. is that the drier subjects just require a greater degree of preparation with the use of real life case studies and anecdotes to highlight the principles of what is being taught. This does require significant research but the rewards are there to be gained.

To create a truly vibrant presentation as much time needs to be spent on case studies, anecdotes and jokes as is spent in the factual aspects of the presentation, and then all of these should be committed to memory. The trainer or speaker who is entirely tied to course notes or slides looks unprofessional, and will inevitably end up being a bore.

2 Have group interaction and engagement

Do you remember the little phrases from earlier in this chapter? The first one really comes into play at this point – "The trainer does not know everything". No one likes to be lectured at. The best trainers and speakers enable the delegates to learn by allowing them to be a part of the process, offering their point of view, and allowing the audience to relate their emotions and experiences to the subject. Training is not a one sided process and people do not absorb information like a computer downloading software. It is an interactive process where information is exchanged.

3 Use humour and fun to create interest and feedback

Surprisingly, many people have thought that training courses and presenting seminars needed to be a serious affair with little space for humour. How wrong could they be? Here's another analogy for you – if you eat a dry meal too quickly you'll suffer with indigestion. So, it stands to reason that if you consume dry information too quickly you'll suffer from "intellectual indigestion". We all suffer very easily with intellectual indigestion from time to time, and definitely need a regular dose of "intellectual antacid" (otherwise known as "humour and fun") to relieve the situation. Failure to relieve the situation will certainly cause violent and uncontrollable bouts of "intellectual flatulence" (or information overload) as the brain tries desperately to redress the balance by expelling everything it's just tried to absorb (roughly translated as "forgetting everything that's just been said").

4 Nurturing

Drawing the delegates out of their shells, allowing them to fully interact and contribute in the session is vital in today's training. Questioning is a fantastic way of achieving this. More on this later.

> *"By the inch it's a cinch by the yard it's hard"*
>
> Napolean Hill

As we have seen, the rules have certainly changed. Utilising the latest techniques and different ways to stimulate and engage the whole group is where this book becomes invaluable. It is not about lesson planning or the technical stuff behind training (though they are important); these are simple techniques that can be applied immediately in your training and presentations to engage your audience.

So, the first task in any training session is to get the delegates interested, open, interacting and consequently ready to learn.

Stop & think

Question 1
What rules are you working under in your present training sessions? Be honest!

Question 2
How many of the rules do you identify with on a regular basis?

Question 3
When was the last time you injected some humour into the session?

Chapter 2

Step 1 Understanding yourself & the group

WHAT ARE YOU like as a speaker or trainer? Are you energised when speaking? Do you physically stand up for the majority of the training session, or walk the room, engaging with each and every delegate, enjoying the interaction? Is it just another day's work, where much of what you do is from the chair (or lectern, or podium) at the front, going through the motions, wishing you were somewhere else? Which of these fits you?

If your energy levels are down, and you can't get them up, how do you expect the group to be engaged? I have experienced this personally many times from speakers and trainers who present induction sessions, who should really know better. It's not a difficult concept, and it's certainly no secret – you get out of a session what you put in.

Stop & think

Try these for size

	Yes	No	Don't know
Do you reach every member of the group?	☐	☐	☐
Do you understand the prefered learning styles of your delegates?	☐	☐	☐
Do you notice when delegates are feeling uncomfortable about the room temperature or layout?	☐	☐	☐
Do you notice if someone is having difficulty with the topic or the subject matter?	☐	☐	☐
Do you ever take notice of the evaluation or feedback forms?	☐	☐	☐
Do you find training difficult and demanding at times?	☐	☐	☐
Do you always know the answer to every question the delegate asks you?	☐	☐	☐

How did you get on? There are no right or wrong answers as they apply solely to you. From the questions though, you should be able to see that success in this area is all about how observant we are and how much we really care for the courses we run and the delegates who attend. Later on we will examine the different types of delegates, but let's just remain observant for a short while longer.

"One of the greatest faults in modern education is over structuring, which does not allow for play at every point in the educational process"

Edward T. Hall

In a lot of cases many trainers and speakers are poor at delivering the message, yet have a thorough understanding of the subject. Others are great at putting the message over but are less knowledgeable about the subject. I can't help you improve your subject knowledge, but spending time observing your group and being sensitive to their needs (including basic housekeeping matters like room temperatures, room layouts, and facilitating regular refreshment and comfort breaks) can pay huge dividends in ensuring they engage and remain focussed on the learning experience.

And above all, your enthusiasm will be contagious. It absolutely doesn't matter what the work related topic is, if you are enthusiastic about it, it will shine through and your delegates will be enthused too.

Understanding Your Group

There are times when you will know some of your delegates, especially if you're facilitating some in-house training. Other times you may not know anyone at all. The same rules apply regardless of this, and we are about to deal with the different types of delegates you might meet.

Now a note must be made at this point that we are only dealing with basic delegate types and the list below is not an exhaustive compendium, but it is intended to give you a broad view of various types of people you will come across. Indeed you will find them in all walks of life.

How many of these types of people do you recognise? Imagine being able to hold, inspire and engage this audience!

The Mobile Person

This person cannot stop looking at their phone. They feel they have to stay in contact with the office or their co-workers, otherwise the job or office will grind to a halt. They even try to send a sneaky text now and again, or might explain to you that they are expecting an important call from the office at any time which they absolutely have to answer.

You need to include this type of person in your presentation from the start, and keep them included throughout the session. You can ask them questions or ask for their comments on different things or even have them do role play with you. Regardless of the method you use, make sure that they are so involved that they do not have time to worry about their ego or their office.

Often such a person is attending under sufferance. The BOSS has said that attendance is compulsory and the delegate believes they do not need to go on the training course. They might have even made comments earlier to work colleagues to that effect. This, more often than not, is the ego speaking, although the root cause may well be deeper seated and involve a fear of academic failure. They may not have been able to grasp concepts at school which they feel embarrassed about, and so view any form of more formal learning experience as a bad thing. They compensate for this by exaggerating the practical aspects of their job which is why they would prefer to be disturbed by "urgent" calls than devote full attention to the course. You would need to adopt a much more interactive approach for this person, and employ the informal and humorous presentation style to put this person at ease.

The Doodler

Many people do this to relax and can still listen without a problem. But others do this because they are bored and have a short attention span. As they doodle they are dreaming about being somewhere else.

Be careful with this type of person. Sometimes they are indeed listening carefully, and just because they tend not to look up much it doesn't mean they are not interested. Many people work this way on training courses, so feel free to ask them the occasional question just to satisfy yourself that all is well, but do not infer that you think they may not be interested. I remember one lady on a course that I gave never looked up or forward at all, but her manager reported to me later how thoroughly she enjoyed the whole course, and was looking forward to implementing the techniques discussed. What causes a person to react in this way?

It could be that they find it comfortable making notes all the time. It could be that they're shy and prefer not to be noticed. Like our "mobile person" it might be through fear of an as yet unknown learning experience. Then again it could be a more practical issue like they have some form of vision impairment and cannot see the slides properly from where they are seated. Another possibility is that they might have a hearing impediment and have difficulty hearing.

Why, in the two latter cases, would they choose to sit in an inconspicuous place at the back of the room? Their impediment might be only very slight but enough to make them shy of other people and sitting at the front may be uncomfortable for them.

There is a need here to be very understanding and compassionate, but do try and get them into a more appropriate position in the group. It is also good practice to try and find out during your introduction if anyone has any difficulty seeing the slides (if you plan to use them) or hearing what you're saying. In this way you immediately imply that you have their best interests at heart without having to say so, and if the delegates are being honest you've eliminated some of the possible reasons why people may appear not to be paying attention before you begin on the main part of your presentation.

It also helps to have full course notes available to take away at the end, so you can announce that no one has to write anything during the presentation.

The Show-off

These people love courses and meetings and like to throw themselves into any activity or debate. They positively leap at the chance to be the first to ask a question, even if they already know the answer. They prefer to show off either in front of their bosses (if they are on the course as well) or other delegates whom they already know, but are more than prepared to share their knowledge with a "new" group in an effort to win them over as well. It's no surprise therefore to learn that show–offs are often very insecure about themselves and have very poor self-worth. Their behaviour is intended to show, through over-friendliness or bravado, that they are confident, knowledgeable, and thoroughly likeable. Regrettably this is not usually the impression that others around them pick up.

Pleasant as it is to have someone enthusiastic and active in the group, they can be very disruptive as well. There are always reasons behind their behaviour and you should try and establish what they are. The key, as always, is to engage with them as quickly as possible, but never ever belittle them. More often than not they behave the way they do because they have very low self esteem and they feel they have to show off to try to better themselves and their standing within the group.

It is all too easy to put such a person "in their place" and "bring them down to size". However, do that and you have fallen into the trap of fighting fire with fire. Their behaviour will become worse and they will be ever more disruptive. If you can gently quiet them down, help to lift their esteem and show that they can be an active player and make a serious contribution to the group without dominating or taking over, then you will be their friend for life and maybe change their whole way of thinking.

The Talker
As the name implies, these people need to talk. They are uncomfortable when asked to be silent or there is silence around them. It is almost an obsession that they have to fill any silence.

These types of delegate can just as easily disrupt the group, as they can bring the group together especially when no one has anything to say. The key as always is to strike a balance, allowing them enough opportunity to contribute but also allowing others to have their say. Likewise the importance of free discussion and breaks needs to be off set by quieter periods of reflection and concentration, especially when you as the presenter need to get key points across without interruption. Identify the Talker early if you can, and when you need to pose a question to the group, ask the talker first, and then move the questions around the group so that you don't single them out too often. Allowing them time to talk will relax them.

The Polarity Responder
These people are frequently what I call "perverted perfectionists". They seem to take great delight in finding something wrong, or just take a polarised or opposing view for no real reason.

I have met more than my fair share of these people, but the good news is they are quite easy to spot. On arrival, they will studiously review all the printed material and be the first to criticise any apparent error or ambiguous statement. Having found such, and be assured they will usually find something; they will immediately seek people with whom they can spread the good news of their excellent powers of discernment to the detriment of the trainer. Comments like, "I didn't expect him to be any good!" or "Can't be much of a trainer if his course notes are like this!" or "Well, I don't expect to get much out of this!" are usual lines in his/her favourite song.

People like this can be very damaging as they will try to disrupt the group and spread negativity. A tell tale sign is that they like to prefix their comments with, "I wouldn't want to cause any trouble but..."

Be on your guard for these delegates, and the minute you see them (even before the meeting starts if possible) you can disarm them by asking if they wouldn't mind studying the course notes carefully because your proof reader was away and it has caused a few copies to go out unchecked. This is a small thing, but immediately makes them feel you value their comments. If they find anything you should thank them profusely and if appropriate even tell the group how much you appreciate their contribution.

The Trouble Maker

Trouble makers are very often akin to the Polarity Responder in that they look to criticise and pick fault, with a smattering of Show-off thrown in for good measure, and are usually set off through boredom. They revel in boring or tiresome sessions and will try to ensure that they disrupt the whole group. If you are not careful, they have the power to destroy the group. This, they believe, shows how clever they are.

They will intentionally raise issues which have nothing to do with the training in hand but will have everything to do with disrupting the flow of the material. They are generally quick witted and clever with words, and under the guise of humour will try to show up the trainer and so elevate themselves from mere delegate to informal leader.

They might decide to ask random questions, like "Does anyone know how the football went last night?" right in the middle of a session on Health and Safety.

If you find you have a trouble maker in your group you must deal with them ruthlessly and quickly. Do not allow any irrelevant or random questions, and make it clear that it is inappropriate to ask them during the session. If it's really necessary to ask, then they can ask someone at the break. Do not under any circumstances debate the issue or tolerate interruptions.

The Nervous Worrier

They are, as the name implies, nervous and worried individuals, and are generally so scared and uncomfortable in a group learning situation that they will not be able to keep up. As a result they fail to understand what is being delivered and only hear a small fraction of what is being said. They are usually quite easy to identify from their body language alone.

Generally this person has never felt that they have succeeded in anything and indeed may have been conditioned from childhood that they can never study or pass exams. Even in our time of enlightenment, we have people like that and you will come across them.

When you spot them, preferably before the session starts, interact with them. Have a chat over coffee and put them at their ease. Reassure them that you won't be singling them out, asking them to do anything strange or irrelevant, or put them in a position where they will be embarrassed or uncomfortable in front of the other delegates.

If they feel happy to help you with the presentation, assuming there are elements that can be handled in this way, get them to come out and assist you. It might be that a more fundamental problem exists that makes them nervous about being in a group situation, like a hearing or visual impairment or dyslexia for example. It's possible therefore, that allowing them to participate "hands on" as your assistant will enable them to integrate into the group and not only learn something for themselves but also provide a valuable contribution to the group as a whole.

The Academic

These people are usually really smart and can project their thinking very quickly. Once they have done this, or think that they have, they quickly become bored and start to switch off.

Academics are usually very good at picking up the theme, but can get bored if the session is constantly slowed down to allow others to keep up. They tend to read all course literature and look at their watch frequently, or anything else that catches their eye. By using carefully selected anecdotes (which we shall explore in Chapter 4 – Step 8, page 77) it is possible to ensure that, from time to time, whilst they might think they know what's coming, they regularly find out that they don't. This tends to ensure that even the most perceptive delegate listens intently.

The Bored Person

This individual (similar to the doodler) simply has a short attention span and gets bored quickly.

This is especially so if they don't find the topic stimulating. They can then go into their own world or even distract the whole group. Here is where a very well planned and structured presentation is absolutely imperative. The price of not having the presentation completely structured is very high.

It should also be mentioned that whilst many of the delegate types listed here manifest themselves as a result of deep seated conditions and personality types, any seemingly engaged and focussed delegate can transform into a Bored Person if the course content is not well prepared, structured or delivered with enthusiasm.

The Dreamer

On a pleasant, quiet, and warm day when you are parked on what we hope is a comfortable chair and the trainer's voice is ever so slightly droning on, it's fair to say that idle minds will wander all over the place.

The Dreamer's favourite music will be wafting through their head, plans for the coming weekend considered, or last weekends activities analysed (or regretted). Possibly, they are trying to solve the problem of how much building material they might need for a forthcoming project, or how to get back into someone's good books.

After lunch this gets worse, and the Dreamer will soon be about three or four minutes behind the rest of the group and the current discussion. Sometimes it is necessary to go back and collect them which slows down the flow of the session and risks others becoming distracted too. In the right circumstances we all have a tendency to daydream, so this kind of behaviour should not be unexpected.

After lunch is a very reliable time for people with day dreaming tendencies to drift off, and the trick to holding on to them is by being a little outlandish. A really good topical joke or comical clip will always work. Everyone has a belly laugh and then you have them back again, dreamers and all. And if you're not the world's best comedian, some kind of physical activity or task can usually keep everyone awake until afternoon break.

The Know it all - they appear in every group.

A brief story about the generic "know it all" with a really good punch line will often curb their tendencies without causing any offence, and the group has a good laugh. A word of caution however; keep all stories general and never at the expense of an individual.

The Questioner

These are people who will question anything and everything including those things that are quite irrelevant to the subject in hand. For example, "I have another question on this. Hypothetically if ..." and sometimes the question isn't related to the topic at all. On the other hand, some people try to catch you out with their well thought out questions, instead of asking them for a genuine reason. To avoid this, make sure that the topic is very well prepared and delivered in a competent and congruent way. This reduces the opportunity for the rogue questioner and when the red herring questions come up you can cut them out straight away.

A quick line about questions. If any delegate happens to catch you with a question that you do not know the answer to, and lets be honest, none of us are perfect or absolutely knowledgeable about everything (don't forget, "The trainer does not know everything") then admit it and offer to come back to them with an answer later. Do not try to debate it in the session as this can lead to huge time wasting and upsets the flow of the presentation.

"It is one of the most beautiful compensations of this life that no man can sincerely try to help another without helping himself"
Ralph Waldo Emerson

Step 2 Ultimate rapport building

BUILDING RAPPORT IS analogous to strengthening a bridge over a river; the stronger the bridge, the more it can carry. That is, the better rapport that you have in a relationship with someone, the more you can ask of them.

So rapport, in this context, is like an invisible bridge or connection between you and an individual or a group of people. It doesn't mean you have to be the best of friends, but it does mean that you feel comfortable in their presence, and vice versa. If you have a group where you do not feel comfortable with one or more then try to involve them as soon as possible. Very likely the discomfort is because they feel threatened, unsure or uncomfortable in some way by you, or you might feel threatened, unsure or uncomfortable in some way by them. So how do we establish a rapport with someone we have only just met? It is easier than you think and involves:

- Using active listening skills to hear what they are saying.
- Making empathetic statements which demonstrate you understand their situation and needs.
- Asking them questions about their views, or the problems they

see, or the reservations they have.

- Finding things that you have in common and talking about them.
- Dealing with them face to face and looking them in the eye.
- Taking an interest in the whole person, and their wider interests, not just their work or the task they are currently working on.
- Remember you are interested in them, so make sure that is how the conversation goes.

"The best conversationalist is the person who says nothing but encourages the other to tell all"

Dr. Arch Hart
Fuller Seminary, Pasadena USA

Why do we need to establish rapport at all? Research suggests that in the absence of rapport, training courses would be flat and to be brutally honest, downright boring. When we establish a connection with the group we can take the course to the next level. Once you establish an emotional bond with your audience you will dramatically enhance their trust and faith in you.

Why build rapport?

Building rapport is about developing a real understanding of the people you are with. It matters not whether they are a group, team or just individuals. It is all about them and you feeling that there is a level of understanding between you.

When you have rapport you can lead people nearly anywhere. As a trainer it is important to have the group go with you and interact as much as possible, then they will respond positively to you.

Matching & mirroring

Mirroring is a human behavior characterised by copying someone else while communicating with them. It is often observed in people exhibiting similar postures, gestures, or tone of voice. It may include miming gestures, movements, body language, muscle tensions, expressions, tones, eye movements, breathing, tempo, accent, attitude, choice of words, metaphors, or other features discernible in communication.

34

Mirroring happens very naturally when people are conversing. The listeners will typically smile or frown along with the speaker talking to them. If one person throws in sports metaphors, another person, who is in rapport and mirroring, will likely carry along similar lines.

It is somewhat like a communication dance. There is matching as if in a dance, while having normal conversation. People do this naturally with their silent body language and spoken words.

When meeting people, if you display the same expression as they have, or mirror their expression, they will generally be much friendlier. You might see this related to the way a person accepts their own image when looking in a mirror.

Without even consciously knowing it, the vast majority of people naturally match and mirror each other's verbal and non verbal cues. Next time you are around people, at a home, conference or meeting, night out, anywhere really, look out for this, phenomenon and you will be surprised at what happens.

Verbal matching is the same principal however with the words, using the speed of the voice, tonality etc. People start to use the same words, at home or at work, again this is mostly unconscious.

I know of a guy who occasionally goes back home to Liverpool from his work in London. He has lived down there for over 20 years but can immediately pick up the accent again subconsciously.

Pacing and leading

Where mirroring is the technique of leading a person through having them copy your body language, Pacing and Leading is the same but based on your verbal and physical communication. In this area you can begin to pace a person's movements even their breathing for a few minutes and then you make the next move and lead with your body language. This is what many professional trainers and sales people do.

In any interaction between two or more people, there is always someone who leads while the others follow. Take a look around in any place where there are groups of people. The next time you're facilitating a training event or seminar, quietly step aside and just observe how people interact at the informal sessions or break times. You will see how some will take a very visible physical stance (the leader) and this will attract others to them. You will see the leader shift their stance slightly and the others will mimic the change. Through unconscious body language, they are affirming that "We're with you."

Now if you really want to reinforce your standing as the facilitator of the seminar, you can move in on a group and watch carefully how the dynamics change. You, as the formal leader, are appointed leader of the seminar and so command a level of respect which the informal leader does not have.

Watch how the group will now orientate to you. The informal leader will do one of two things. They will;

- either move away from the group, a gesture of defeat and passing the authority to you, or
- remain in the group and try to challenge you for the right to lead the group. You might be the formal leader but this is outside your jurisdiction. After the break is over you are leader again but now a challenge could occur.

It is happening all around us. Children look like and talk like their parents. Everyone wants the adulation of the group and so from our childhood, we have learnt how to achieve this. We learn it from our parents and other adults or older siblings around us. Mimicking their body language is possibly the most common way.

Now that you are aware of the effect that pacing and leading can have, it is up to you to use this technique to help mould your delegates into a coherent group. That is, one where everyone feels included and comfortable.

Your primary target is to ensure that before anything else, you mould your delegates into a coherent, vibrant, focussed group. It should be possible to do this in the first session. However, if the course spans a number of days you can have the luxury of welding them together through the first day. Just remember one very important thing, **IT MUST BE DONE**.

If someone talks fast, try to increase the speed of your voice to match them; if they talk more slowly then try to match this as well. Do this carefully though, in a way that is unconscious to the speaker, otherwise it'll seem that you're actually making fun of them.

Since the meaning of any communication is the response you get, it is imperative that you know what type of delegate you have, so that you can respond appropriately.

Always make sure that what you mean to say is what the group actually hears you say. What does that mean?

Take any group of people and then make a statement, something a little dramatic, maybe slightly shocking, or perplexing, but certainly something open to interpretation. Then ask the members of the group to re-tell what they just heard you say. It's important that they don't say back word for word what you've just said, but what they thought you meant by it. You'll be surprised that a lot of the group will have interpreted what you said in ways you never imagined. Obviously be sure that you speak in English (or the common language of the group) but always make sure that what they hear is actually what you mean.

For further reading on this checkout, Nick Owen's book The Magic of Metaphor, and then include the Kinaesthetic by passing around a short message i.e. Chinese whispers, or tapping out some tune.

Music works very well in much the same way. Try playing some soft classical music before your presentation and just see the calming effect it has on both you and your group.

What is your representational system?

Have you ever heard someone say *"Picture this"*, or *"That sounds great"*, or *"I'm not sure how I feel about that"*? These phrases fall into different categories of representational systems which we call *"modes"*, and people use a preferred mode in their understanding and use of language.

According to research carried out in the 1970's by Dr Richard

Bandler and Dr John Grinder, when developing Neuro Linguistic Programming (NLP), everyone will use a mixture of the communication modes but also tend to favour one mode over the others. For example, some people like to think in pictures, visualising situations or problems, and they do this throughout their day instinctively. This doesn't mean that they don't use the other modes; it's just that their preferred representational system is visual.

The three basic types of representational system (modes) are;

1 Visual
2 Auditory
3 Kinaesthetic (feelings)

1 The Visual trainer or delegate will use sentences like;
Do you see what I mean?
This looks good
I see where you're going with this idea
That person has a bright future ahead of them
Picture this for an idea
Let's focus on this issue
I have this great vision
Let me show you
I have a great view

Visual trainers tend to talk faster and can be somewhat excited, generally moving around the training room instead of remaining at the front and using their arms/hands and whole body to express their feelings or themes within the presentation.

Some of you may remember Professor Magnus Pike, the eccentric scientist, and the way he used his arms as he got increasingly excited when explaining things, even drawing pictures of things right out in front of him.

"The soul never thinks without a picture"

Plato

2 The Auditory trainer or delegate will use sentences like;
Hear me out
How does that sound to you?
Don't take that tone with me
That rings a bell
I will give you a call
I hear you loud and clear
I'm just sounding you out
This sounds great
Sound the alarm
He left shouting and screaming

Auditory trainers tend to rely on their voice more than the use of body language, and like to use tonality to create expression. They also tend to stand in one position throughout their training or speech – many politicians do this.

3 The Feeling (kinaesthetic) trainer or delegate will use sentences or words like;
This can be handled easier with some revision
The group usually grasped new ideas
It all boils down to one thing
The task weighed heavily on him
We need to build a firm foundation
I am burdened with all this
I want you to nail down

Kinaesthetic trainers think from the heart, and usually give a good balanced presentation; they use some body language especially when passionate about a topic. Do you know anyone who is passionate about their topic (i.e. a kinaesthetic person, but also uses a lot of voice tonality and timbre)?

An understanding of the different communication modes is important, and is a key element in building rapport quickly with a group of people you've only just met. By allowing your delegates to introduce themselves at the start of a session, and asking open ended questions that encourage them to talk, you can pick up, by listening intently to them, what type of person they are (visual, auditory or kinaesthetic). Then, when you are presenting a training session, if you have identified the different types of people in the room correctly, and you can get to know their preferred style, you can blend and weave a beautifully fluid session where you effectively train a group together but with the power of a one to one.

This is an incredibly powerful technique, the effect of which should never be underestimated.

Another very easy but equally powerful technique for building rapport is to start using the delegates' first name as soon as you can in the presentation. This draws them in, especially the ones who feel that they don't want to be there. Use this technique often, especially if someone appears to be daydreaming. More about this in Step 9.

Personally speaking, I like to start learning about the people on my courses and seminars as soon as they arrive on the first day. I always make a point of using the first half an hour of the course as an informal networking session over coffee (usually with some pastries and other tasty treats, especially if it's an early start) so that everyone can relax. Some people will be nervous about meeting others, some may have had a bad journey in, and some may have struggled to find the venue or get parked. So a gentle start to the day is always a good idea, and it allows for time to personally meet and greet every delegate, and if required introduce those who don't know anyone else to the rest of the group.

Now, it obviously helps to have a good memory, and there are many good books that can help you achieve this if yours isn't as good as you'd like it to be; but being able to relate on a very simple but personal level to everyone in the room right from the start will get the session off on the right foot. I also like to get the delegates to introduce themselves to the group at the start of the formal session, which is made much easier for those who are nervous about speaking in front of people if you've had the informal warm up beforehand. And if you've done your work correctly over coffee, you might already know a few details about your delegates that link them together – a few may have similar hobbies for example, so you can link people in this way as you move from one to another. Little touches like this can make a huge difference to the start of the course, where everyone feels welcome and part of the event.

Another variation on the pacing and leading techniques that can help build rapport, is that of mirroring. This can be done either through verbal communication or physical (body language). As I mentioned previously, this is especially valuable when meeting people who favour the auditory or visual communication modes, although kinaesthetic people will be able to pick up on both. For auditory people, try to learn to instinctively change the tonality and speed of your voice to match theirs, although please be subtle. Try it on a couple of delegates who talk noticeably fast or slow, or someone who you feel doesn't want to be there, being very careful that they do not feel you are making fun of them.

Another profound thing you can do which will be effective for visual people is to mirror the individual's body movements when interacting with them. This may seem like a tall order, but we all do this instinctively when we interact with each other. To prove this, sit two people back to back and ask them to talk about their last holiday for 4 to 5 minutes, and watch what happens. The same body language will be adopted by both people, with either arms or legs crossed in the same way.

Stop & think

Question
What sort of words or language do you use when you're in a training session?

Rapport level indicator

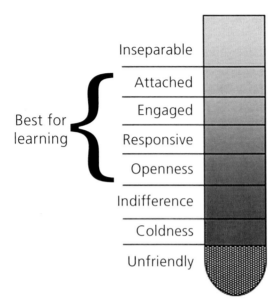

Inseparable

Attached

Engaged

Best for learning {

Responsive

Openness

Indifference

Coldness

Unfriendly

source: Eric Jensen

"To speak ill of others is a dishonest way of praising ourselves"
Will Durant

Despite all the theory, building and establishing rapport is mostly done unconsciously. Although the delegates will eventually establish a rapport among themselves in their own time, you can speed the process up by leading the activity yourself. Using the techniques outlined above, try to get a group fully engaged by the afternoon of the first day of a course.

To really get to know how they think and react, you must know something about them. This is why the preliminary research needs to be done early on, and can be achieved by asking questions about their life, home and work. Remember another golden rule - to be interesting, you must be interested.

For someone to be interested in you, you have to make sure that you are interested in what they are saying first. Give them time to talk about themselves, ask questions which allow them to provide more information, and don't interrupt in order to say what you think before they've finished explaining what they think.

They do not need to know about you, and so you should

endeavour to listen to every delegate when making a presentation. Every time I relate something back to an individual's own environment you can actually see their understanding improve, and their respect and confidence grows because you have paid attention to them. At the same time you might actually learn something about their work environment as well.

"Once a human being has arrived on this earth, communication is the largest single factor determining what happens to him"
Virginia Satir

Another little tip - **NEVER** say "No" or dismiss in an off-hand way a question posed from the delegates, or belittle an answer someone has given to a question you have asked. There is a good reason for this. It might be that you want to understand exactly what level of knowledge the group currently has, so asking technical questions might do this more quickly. It is advisable however, to begin with what you consider to be quite simple questions first and gradually develop them. In doing this you start from a point of common knowledge and build on the knowledge. Doing this also helps to develop the camaraderie within the group, and confidence of the individuals.

You begin to feel the atmosphere in the room lift and more delegates get involved. This is crucial to running a fantastic programme. Be careful not to get dragged down or off the topic though, especially from the Show Off or Time Waster delegates. You can explain that you will be covering "such and such" a topic later or that the question relates to something that's not part of the syllabus, without offending anyone or halting the flow of the course. If it's something useful, then you always have the option of discussing it with the delegate during breaks or lunch, if you think it's necessary.

We absorb information and learn by using all our senses, visual, auditory and the emotional and through our conscious thinking and subconscious thinking. You should not be discouraged from using all the senses but always be aware that although you might set off a good memory for someone, you might inadvertently trigger a painful memory for someone else.

"The true aim of everyone who aspires to be a teacher should be not to impart his own opinions but to kindle minds"

Frederick Robertson

Naturally it's impossible to safeguard against every eventuality, but it's best to carefully think of what you are going to say before you say it. One manager was seen to place a sign about his desk which read; ENGAGE BRAIN BEFORE OPENING MOUTH.

The use of real life stories, plenty of movement to generate energy in the room, combined with the use of rich voice tonality with full engagement from the group will always help develop the group and lead to a successful session. Once you get everyone engaged and on board, you can then lead them where you need to go, and the time seems to fly by. You can tell when you are going in the right direction because people will be willing to participate and won't even think about the time. Once you achieve this momentum and you feel the delegates are with you, the rest of the course will run smoothly.

I recall a guy who came to speak to a group, and the subject was a pretty boring and a technical topic. He assumed we ought to know the technical information, and it didn't once occur to him to ask if we actually did. Well, we didn't. Consequently within 30 minutes he had completely lost us; the course went way above the heads of the vast majority of people in the room, and for me, it resulted in a complete waste of time.

Many years ago while doing some joint training with another trainer, a major point was made by telling someone in the room that they were wrong, in a rather harsh tone – "No that's not right!" For the rest of the course the delegate steadily dropped down the rapport indicator to a very low level and I felt the energy in the room fall because of this. As ever, it had a contagious effect on the rest of the group.

The worrying thing was the other trainer seemed completely unaware of how his words had affected the individual, and simply carried on ploughing through the syllabus. What's worse was that this course lasted four days and the rapport with the delegate was never regained.

If for some reason you make a blunder, and we are only human after all, be sincere and humble enough to apologise and ask for forgiveness. It is the only way to repair such a blunder.

Banter keeps people motivated and attentive. The vast majority of people pay a lot more attention because they're having fun and interacting.

Dan Terry

Step 3 It's all in the voice

H OW MANY COURSES or presentations have you attended where the topic excites you and you are looking forward to it, but the presenter (who is an expert in their field), lets the whole thing down with a dull and monotonous voice? In those cases, don't you find that trying to concentrate only makes it worse?

Some people do have voices that are heavy and authoritarian, just as there are some which are easy to listen to. From the presenter's perspective this has very little to do with whether you are actually interesting, but everything to do with how well prepared you are.

I believe the sound of our voice as a trainer is a very important tool. When words are combined with tonality and body language they can deliver a powerful message.

How much of your communication is about the words we use?

Can I make my voice more interesting? The answer is yes, just by working on your tonality alone can have startling results......

"Sticks and stones can break my bones, but words can break my heart"

Robert Fulghum

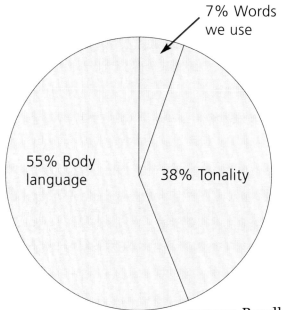

7% Words
we use

55% Body
language

38% Tonality

source: Bandler & Grinder

First and foremost, no matter how good you think you are at presenting and being understood, you should get a video camera and film yourself leading a session. This will help even if it's a practice session that is being recorded. Once you have the DVD, play it all the way through and see yourself as your delegates see you. Be as critical as possible about your own performance, and make a list of everything you believe that you have done wrong.

Write down what you liked about your presentation. Then write down what you didn't like. Make a note of how you could change

Stop & think

What does your voice sound like?
What voice irritates the hell out of you and why?
Do you think your voice is monotonous or full of wonderful tonality?
Can you tell a great story and have people listen to every word?

These may be simple questions but they're important and need to be considered.

the things you didn't like, and apply them to the whole presentation. Having gone through your whole presentation, do the filming and critical analysis exercise all over again. Keep repeating this cycle until you are perfectly happy with the result and believe that you would find yourself interesting and a pleasure to listen to if you were in the audience.

Looking back to the pie chart above, only 7% of what we convey is done through the words we speak. The remainder is conveyed through our body language and tonality.

1 Inflection of your voice

Some people who use a lot of inflection or modulation at the end of a line or the sentence so it always sounds like a question, an example of this would be – have you finish-ed that job yet? Are your feel- ing affected by this news? Do you have any infor-mation about the train times? However sometimes people sound like they are asking a questions due to the inflection of their speech on a regular basis, which in training can have an advantage if you want delegates to be involved and a disadvantage if you have several talker/show offs slowing the whole day down: listen out for this.

"Sometimes it's not what you say that's important in training, it's the way you say it"

Children are especially good at this, and generally know that when they ask for a favour they can detect by the sound of your voice if you really mean NO, because a lot of the communication is also in the body language and the tonality of the words used.

Stop & think

Can you think of how many ways a person can say NO?
Here is a simple exercise:
With words, tonality and body language, always remembering that sometimes NO can really mean Yes (more on that later), see how many ways you can say NO and yet mean different things.

2 Tonality

This refers to your vocal pitch (high and low notes). For example, when people get excited the pitch of their voice goes higher, when they're making a serious point it drops low, and in general conversation or training the flow goes up and down from high to low and back again. I use this variation in tonality a lot in training, as I find it keeps the group fully engaged, especially when the topic can seem a little dry, or we're suffering through a warm graveyard shift – i.e. the session after lunch.

3 Timbre

This refers to the distinctive character of the voice apart from its pitch and intensity, and can be used to great effect when recalling stories and anecdotes. I referred in part to this in a previous chapter. When I have a room full of delegates it's possible that some may have the same first name, so I make a point of saying these names in a different timbre for each person. When mixed with changes in tonality this has a fantastic effect in keeping everybody engaged and involved, and it also generates laughter and interest.

Does your voice sound different when you are excited or enthusiastic about a particular topic? It should! I always make a point of getting in an elevated or excited state before a training session. From experience I know this can be very contagious.

I remember going to see an international motivational speaker a few years ago, and he came on stage in a heightened motivational mood and within minutes the audience were following this mood, the atmosphere was electric, and you could feel the energy in auditorium.

Many training courses over the years have been very dry because no real effort has been made by the trainer to bring the subject area alive. For some people that is just their style, and they are totally oblivious to the fact that they are boring. Sometimes the trainer could have lost interest in the topic, and some people believe they are doing a fine job.

If you think that this might be you, and you are not getting the response you would like to have from your delegates, go back and remake your DVD to see what the problem is.

It's fair to say at this point that many people have never been trained as a trainer. Holding a degree or PhD in a subject has always been considered enough to indicate that you were totally equipped and gifted to teach the subject. Thankfully this view is not widely held nowadays, and more and more trainers have had some form of training before stepping out in front of an audience. Naturally there are some professions where the trainers have to convey lorry loads of facts and statistics, and it may be very difficult to lighten the mood of this type of presentation. However, with good preparation any subject can be presented in such a way that it is interesting and engaging.

It has to be noted though, that some people do like this style of learning, but they are few and far between.

It does not matter what the topic is – Health and Safety, accountancy, or the finer points of watching paint dry, you can make it worthwhile so the delegates can take something away, just by using the tone of your voice or including some interesting facts and appropriate anecdotes. Every presentation can have a profound effect if you plan and present it well. There is a great website on facts which you would do well to consult. See the bibliography section.

Body language

Sometimes people's body language can be important, but I tend not to concentrate on the body language in isolation. You must consider other factors like the environment (is the room too hot, too cold, nicely comfortable, etc), the topic itself, any conflicts between departments or managers or co-workers that might influence a persons stance. When analysing body language it is imperative that you take all these aspects into account.

But remember, just one aspect of body language does not tell a whole story anymore than one word on a page does.

Just because someone has their arms folded, it doesn't mean they are not interested, it doesn't automatically mean they are feeling negative, and it doesn't necessarily mean that they feel insecure or threatened in your presence. It could be that they're cold.

So, you will need to use all of the different communication elements together, and for that you'll need congruency type training to accurately read the body language. People in politics use symmetry or congruent body language all the time, e.g. Gordon Brown and Tony Blair both use it, with their hands and arms moving in symmetry to the words they are speaking. Watch anyone who speaks {passionately} and you will see it.

When a session gets under way, try and notice the energy in the room; how would you gauge it? Your job will be to raise this energy and engage the whole group. Some people more than others enjoy the involvement, however some don't. You will pick this up almost instinctively with a little practice.

Excellent places to practice reading body language are bus depots, airports or train stations, where you can watch people coming and going. Watch the body language to see how people react when they first see each other, and then as they physically meet and embrace. Contrast this by going to the departure lounge and watch them as they separate and say goodbye. Do this for a while and you will learn how to read people. If you can go with a friend and then compare notes afterwards, then this is even better. These are invaluable experiences and are heartily recommended.

Here are a few simple exercises for you to try out and test your skills.

Through body language we can completely contradict what we are saying verbally. We say one thing, but our body language tells a different story. It's important therefore, in order to be fully clear and understood that we make sure our audible communication and our body language are congruent. Possibly of even greater importance however, is that we become good readers of our delegate's body language.

Let us consider the delegate who is sitting in front of you but constantly playing with his or her fingers. They never look at you and appear quite uncomfortable. The body language could be telling you any number of things. What do you think is being expressed?

As the delegate is talking to you, he or she is constantly placing his/her hand over their mouth. What do you think that might indicate to you?

As your delegate is talking he or she is constantly playing with an ear lobe. What might that mean?

A male has his legs tightly crossed and his arms folded across his chest as he tells you that there is nothing that could possibly frighten him. What is he really saying?

A woman has her legs crossed and then wraps one foot around one leg. At the same time she has her handbag firmly clasped in front of her. She is verbally saying that she is quite comfortable in your presence. Is she lying?

Chapter 3

Step 4 Using visualisation techniques

"Develop success from failures. Discouragement and failure are two of the surest stepping stones to success"

Dale Carnegie

ONE OF THE most powerful things I did when I first started presenting and training, was to visualise the most fantastic presentation, in as much detail as I could. I would see the smiling faces and people leaning forward, interested in everything I said. I realised I needed to feel good about myself, and have confidence in my own ability to lead a group of people on a journey of discovery. By taking time to imagine this, I could actually influence the way I gave a presentation for real. Visualising in this way can be a very powerful technique for improvement, and if used on a regular basis can have a profound affect on your performance and effectiveness.

As a self improvement technique, take 15 minutes or so in a morning every time you have a presentation or more regularly if you prefer, and just sit or lie down quietly and run through the whole presentation in your mind from start to finish. If it's a long training course, running over three or four days for example, then speed it up a bit. It's great fun. And remember the 3 'A's: Awkward, Applying it, and Automatic (source: Sam Horn).

Stop & think

Exercise

Find somewhere quiet, and sit back and relax. Think about your next training or coaching session, and imagine all the people in the room smiling and eager to learn. Go round each one and picture their face. Notice how happy they are to be there, on your course. Notice the colour scheme in the room, the layout and the furniture. Hear the sound of laughter, and notice how eloquently you are handling questions from the group, and how conversation is free flowing both ways, as if you were sailing along. I know if you haven't done this before you will be thinking, *"What's the point?"* However, I want you to remember the following phrase *'What you think about, you bring about'*.

Next notice how good you feel and how lucky you are to be training these wonderful people, feel how comfortable the room is, just the right temperature and just the right amount of sunlight, with everybody learning and asking questions. Let your mind wander and consider the truly positive things about this course. Your unconscious will store all this information as though the course has gone ahead already.

Can you remember the first time you tried to tie your shoelaces, or when you first got in a car to learn to drive? Awkward, to say the least. But you kept on applying it, and eventually it became automatic. Remember when you fell off your bike and you got back on again? Do you remember being told by the person teaching you to ride your bike that if you keep on trying you'll get there in the end? The same principal is at work here. Awkward at first, Applying it, Automatic.

Think back to the phrase I gave you earlier "what you think about, you bring about". How many times have you had butterflies in your stomach, worrying about what questions you are going to be asked, and wondering whether everyone is enjoying the course or not?

It is always a pleasant surprise when training sessions and presentations go a lot better than you expected. After all the nervousness keeps you on your toes, even if you have over prepared, it's a good thing to feel a little nervous.

If you think you are beaten, you are.
If you think you dare not, you don't.
If you'd like to win, but think you can't,
It's almost a cinch you won't.
Life's battles don't always go to the stronger or faster man,
But sooner or later the man who wins
Is the one who thinks he can.

Anon

It is estimated that we have around 60,000 thoughts a day. Most of these are unconscious ones, but we can direct or influence many of these by visualising what we want to happen during our presentation or training session– rather than what we don't want.

The trouble is most people tend to think about what could go wrong. It's amazing how many people I come across when delivering the "Training the Trainer" programme, that wallow in negative thoughts. They're beaten before they even start. I remember one person who said her company had sent her on the course even though she knew she couldn't do this. "How do you know this?" I asked. She replied, "I gave a speech at the company's merger and didn't do very well at all". From then on she believed that she could not do it. With her permission I suggested we explore this within the group. I asked if it is possible that when we do something for the first time there will be an element of nerves, and it will feel considerably awkward (going back to the 3 A's). Everyone agreed that this was highly likely. One of the things we did on the course was establish what it actually was that made her feel like this. She said that for days before she actually gave the speech, which involved presenting to the whole organisation, she would have difficulty sleeping. Consequently this had a knock on effect at work putting her under more stress and anxiety. This is unfortunately very common in today's work environment.

I asked her what specifically she was worried about, and she said that just getting up in front of all the people, and seeing them all looking at her waiting for her to speak, was frightening. She

imagined their eyes as being much larger than normal, and all of them staring forward straight at her, ready to pounce.

In order to help her we ran through some powerful techniques over the next 45 minutes, basically to view these fears in a different way, and remove them from her mind. Her habit of seeing things from the worst possible perspective was actually bringing more of those negative things into her daily training life. It's no surprise that she found standing in front of the audience difficult, because that's what she had already told herself it would be like.

If you have trouble visualising things, you can practice by looking at a photograph or a painting and recalling it piece by piece. The vast majority of people can visualise to some degree, but sometimes the brain processes things so fast you can't remember all the detail straight away. The brain is like a muscle and needs to be trained. I tend to see things as pictures much of the time relatively quickly, so I have to slow things down in order to remember them. Practice makes perfect.

'You never get a second chance
to make a good first impression'

So to make a fantastic first impression, visualise the situation or presentation or talk, and walk yourself through it as positively and thoroughly as you can. If you have already presented a seminar or talk to your audience, and it didn't perhaps go as well as you would have wanted, then you can surprise them all by giving them a far more polished presentation this time.

By studying some of this material, and adopting some of these techniques, the preparation you put in will make a massive difference. See if you can visualise the following things. This will allow your brain to prepare for what's coming next. You can see, hear and feel a presentation going fantastically well. Do this before your next presentation, get comfortable and remember, your delegates are more bothered about how much you care, than how much you know.

1 See your group smiling and enjoying themselves
2 See them sat forward and interested
3 See them looking at you and paying full attention
4 Hear the flow and clarity of your voice
5 Hear yourself answering questions in a competent manner
6 Hear laughter and enjoyment in the room
7 Feel fantastic in yourself
8 Feel relaxed in your style
9 Feel confident

"Life expands or contracts in proportion to one's courage"

Anais Nin

How did you get on? I know at first your mind will wander, and you'll be thinking "What am I trying to do here?", but please, if you do nothing else from this book, keep doing this. It's a well known fact that much of what we worry about is never that bad after all, and the majority of the worry and anxiety is really only in your head. How many times have you worried over nothing?

> *"We have nothing to fear but fear itself"*
> Franklin D Roosevelt

Watch and study some comedy performances. Many of the timing tricks and one-liner's can be incorporated in your own training sessions. When I'm preparing a course or presentation I study the material I need to put across, and then work out how to weave stories, jokes and anecdotes into this. I imagine a thread running through the material, the stories and the group (more on this in a later chapter)

I am passionate about making the training interesting and fast flowing. I have spent many, many hours studying how to improve different types of presentations.

> *"It is well known that what we put into life*
> *is what we get out of it"*

Step 5 Accelerated learning

ACCELERATED LEARNING TECHNIQUES have been around for many years, and they are proving increasingly popular with many trainers, speakers and teachers.

Everyone has a preferred learning style; a way of learning that suits us best. If you know and use the techniques that match your preferred way of learning, you learn more naturally. Because it is more natural for you, it becomes easier. And because it is easier, it is quicker. For once the name for this actually fits the technique, Accelerated Learning. By incorporating memory techniques, Accelerated Learning makes learning an enjoyable, successful and satisfying experience.

Twenty years ago, I don't think the process of accelerated learning was even considered. Sometimes adults who attended some of my courses had been told years before, while still in school that they had some kind of learning issue and wouldn't get very far. Nowadays we can see that it was more likely the education system or more fundamentally, the teacher, wasn't flexible enough to tailor the learning experience or didn't understand (or even know about) different learning styles. This is clearly not the current way of thinking, but it is doubtful whether even highly educated people have been taught any learning techniques or thinking skills, and I doubt that anyone really knows what their preferred learning style is.

This is frustrating because in training we must endeavour to help people get over this barrier to learning. The training programme or course you develop must create a positive learning environment, and incorporate all the techniques you can, i.e. PowerPoint/OHP, posters, flipchart activities, case studies, working groups, use of stories and anecdotes, and the delegates actively giving feedback in their own preferred style. It can be, and is being done, very competently in many places.

Many trainers and speakers are very sequential, analytic and unfortunately fixed in their delivery. Today's trainers and speakers need to reach all of the audience by providing variety, choice, interaction and fun and be able to accelerate the learning process especially in companies that need their staff on the jobs they are paid to do.

The human brain does not have a single learning style we use many styles; delegates are far more complex than that so accelerated learning tends to be;

- Joyful and fun rather than serious and time pressured.
- Activity - based rather than read off the PowerPoint slides.
- Nurturing rather than totally controlling the group
- Flexible rather than a rigid syllabus
- Multi pathed rather than a single path
- Story Telling rather than just going through each slide
- Collaborative rather than competitive
- Results based rather than time based

If you can blend these concepts into your daily training/seminars, you will awaken the delegates to their full learning potential making it enjoyable, it's not a difficult process it's like anything the more planning goes into something the more they and you get out of it. This is what sets the top trainers and speakers apart from the mediocre in the field.

Competence Levels

Let's look at Competence Levels of learning. Why? Because it's very important in training, as we shall see:

There are 4 levels of competence; unconsciously incompetent, consciously incompetent, consciously competent, and unconsciously competent. This sounds highly confusing, but it's really quite straight forward.

When you started to drive a car and got your learners permit or provisional drivers licence, you were no doubt overwhelmed with just how much you needed to remember. There are the controls, foot positioning, mirrors, the steering, not to mention the slight disorientation of controlling a vehicle at speed and watching out for other road users, so much to do at once. Your level of competence in driving was at the unconsciously incompetent level, where you simply don't know what you don't know, and aren't aware of the things you need to know. As a result you were probably quite scared of all the things you would have to do, even though you weren't entirely sure what they were.

As your learning progressed (and this usually happens quite quickly) you became consciously incompetent, in that you now

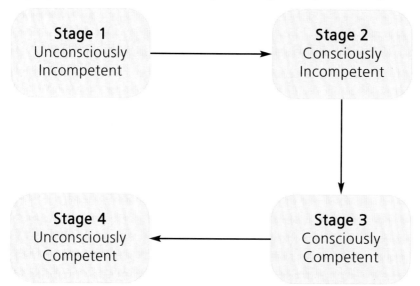

know without any doubt that you are not a very good driver. You are consciously aware that you do not yet know how to drive.

Over time you developed into a good driver, which means that you are now consciously competent and hopefully you passed your driving test. You are aware that you are a good enough driver to pass your test and can confidently drive yourself and your friends around. You're still aware of everything around you though and are careful to drive properly. You are consciously aware of how to drive and have gained knowledge of the road as well as experienced some of the behaviour of other road users.

Finally over a period of time, driving becomes automatic or unconsciously competent. You no longer have to consciously think about changing through the gears, or watching out for pedestrians and cyclists. You can drive and also perform a whole host of other things, like listening to music or chatting with friends in the car. However, becoming unconsciously competent does have other issues associated with it – like complacency. Sometimes a small element of fear keeps us alert and motivated, although we all loose this from time to time.

"It is magnificent to be truly understood and sheer delight when actions are followed through back in the workplace"

Dan Terry

Relating this to training and captivating your audience

When we do our first training session, most of us are nervous and don't quite know how it's going to end up. Whether you cover all the material or not, someone is bound to ask a question you're not sure about. In this case, be honest if you don't know the answer, but always get back to them with the information.

We need to take the audience through this learning process as well. We need them to be competent and have the skills and knowledge they were expecting to learn. But one thing is more important than that, action! I have heard it said that "knowledge is power". Well, knowledge isn't power if it's not used or applied. It's possible that after going through the training we may need to encourage the group to change their ways of working.

Far too often, people come along to courses and seminars with preconceived ideas of what the course or presentation is going to be like. The general view may well be that all training is "boring and irrelevant", especially if the delegate is busy at work and is facing days of problems or catching up when they get back. We have to change that perception, and ensure that everyone feels the learning experience has been worth the time and effort of attending.

If we believe in blending and tailoring the learning process, then where we have heavy subjects like Health and Safety, it is important that humour and other lighter elements form part of the process. Not just jokes and funny anecdotes but also some fun participation on the part of the delegates. Training does not have to be just you, standing in front of a group. Small group workshops can be very informative and a lot of fun. Varying the format of the course will help to develop and maintain the energy and enthusiasm of the group.

There is no such thing as a poor learner. But, there are poor trainers. Remember, a good tradesman never blames their tools for their mistakes.

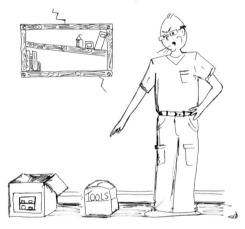

Energy levels in a room, or amongst a group of delegates can be categorised into various levels, ranging from Level 0 (sleep inducing) to Level 5 (full interaction).

The level at which your delegates are at is to a large extent dependent on you. If you are dull and boring then you will be down around level one. As the presentation of your material improves in interest so you will move your delegates up through the levels. Ideally you should strive to get them up to level 4 and 5. When you achieve this you can really feel the energy in the room and no one will be looking at their watch, time will just fly by, it's a fantastic feeling and very rewarding to you and the group.

How can you achieve levels 4 and 5? Simply by applying the steps that are presented in this book but the most important of all is PREPARATION, PREPARATION, and then even more

PREPARATION. You cannot be over prepared for a presentation but you can very easily be under prepared.

How could level 0 to 5 training manifest itself?

Level 0

    1 Dry and dull
    2 Boring
    3 Monotonous speech
    4 Trainer has lost interest
    5 Death by PowerPoint
    7 Topic really boring
    8 Only one or two listening

Level 1

    1 Speakers having difficulty delivering
    2 Message not that clear
    3 Time is dragging
    4 Trainer not experienced with topic
    5 Auditory – likes sound of own voice
    6 Old teaching style

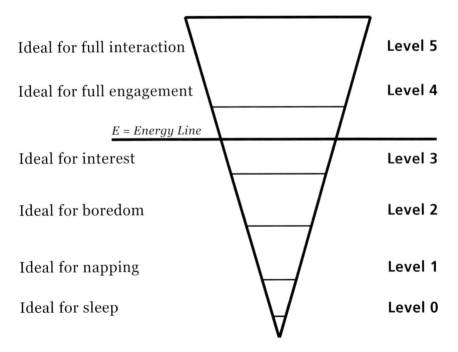

Ideal for full interaction	Level 5
Ideal for full engagement	Level 4
E = Energy Line	
Ideal for interest	Level 3
Ideal for boredom	Level 2
Ideal for napping	Level 1
Ideal for sleep	Level 0

Level 2

1 Could be interesting
2 Speaker wanders
3 Not following a handout
4 Limited interaction
5 Energy feels low

Level 3

1 Doing something practical
2 Involvement
3 Some participating
4 Bursts of energy

Levels 4 - 5

1 Feel the energy in the room
2 Where has the time gone
3 Don't want it to end
4 Fully involved with group
5 Ability to command full attention
6 Full interaction from all
7 Time flies by

Like anything worth doing it takes a little planning and time to achieve the higher levels. As mentioned, preparation is the key to a good presentation and every presentation should be prepared and studied as if it were your first ever presentation. Never become complacent. Complacency, through familiarity, is the most dangerous pit fall you can encounter. We owe it to the delegates to give them the best learning experience ever. It may be we have delivered the same course over a thousand times but you should still regard it as the first time and for most of your delegates, it will be the first time they will have heard it.

Step 6 Two ears one mouth

HAVE YOU EVER heard the expression "*two ears and one mouth*"? We should listen twice as much as we speak; strong listening skills are essential for a trainer. You may be ineffective as a trainer if you don't have effective listening skills; potentially listening skills can inspire others.

Another question; Is it true that some people are better listeners than others? I believe it is.

Did you know, the word "Listen" contains exactly the same letters as the word "Silent"? Both of these contain the same letters as "Enlist". And for good reason.

So to Listen, you need to be Silent, and Enlist both ears. Just doing this one thing during your training session makes a profound difference to the session and will take the training and your understanding of the group to a higher level.

For some people in a big organisation, coming to this training session may be the only platform for them to be heard. For most of their normal working day very few people listen to their problems, concerns or challenges. It is surprising how many decisions are made without consulting or listening to the people who will be directly affected. No wonder many organisations today suffer with low morale and their staff feel like mushrooms. Kept in the dark and fed on, well, you know what!

"The best minute I can invest is the one I invest in people"

Ken Blanchard
The One Minute Manager

Listening

Listening effectively is a skill that every presenter/trainer must develop. For some, it is a natural talent, but for others, it is a skill that must be learned. Sometimes you would like to say that the delegate's situation is not as bad as he/she thinks it is, so you tell a story to out-do theirs. Such an action shows that you have no empathy or feeling with the pain the delegate is experiencing.

To the delegate, his/her pain is the greatest there is and possibly could ever be. While we must not condone self-pity we do have to listen for the real pain and take it seriously. That pain, which may be buried deep inside, is what has to be drawn out.

You must hear every word that is spoken and carefully frame your response to ensure that you draw out what you feel the delegate is trying to say. This may be easy or difficult. It may take one attempt and it might take a number of attempts, but you must show gentleness in how you do this.

Your listening should not just be to the spoken word but also to the body language, which the delegate uses. It has been said that only one third of the information we convey is through the spoken word. The other two thirds of what we say are through our body language. This must not be ignored otherwise we will lose much of what is being expressed.

Information gathering

Having said all this, we must now ensure that we appropriately deal with the information which we have received. We must deal with this in a sensitive manner that will help the delegate through their problem. But, for them, it is to take a step out into the unknown. It is an adventure, which for so many can be frightening. An in-built fear of change did not just happen but was born out of all the experiences of life to date.

This fear, which, you the trainer, will have to deal with, is very real and while you may be able to see past the problem, the delegate cannot. Do not try to make light of fear but help him/her to take the first step.

The first step

There are many ways in which you can help a person take that initial step. First of all, be empathetic with what the delegate is facing. If you have had the advantage of following a similar course you may be able to share your experience and it may be an advantage but remember that the delegate will find it hard to identify with your experience, although you can readily identify with theirs. The delegate is on this adventure for the first time, which for you is familiar territory. You should not be hurt if your experience is rejected as irrelevant.

Danger of "Transference"

In the process of losing the fears, the delegate, may have had, may become or try to become co-dependent on you. If you have been able to limit, minimise or help overcome a situation the delegate has lived with for many years you will have become their absolute hero. This is called transference. Although you should not encourage transference, you should be available to the delegate. The delegate should not feel as if they are on their own but have a secure support to lead them through. It may not always be possible for you individually to provide such a support, which can be extremely time consuming. Here you might like to try and find someone who you feel might be able to provide ongoing nurturing or some other study programme to help them continue on their journey.

Just because you have experienced transference, do not think that you are some super hero. The process is the same as many people experience when seriously ill in hospital and they feel they are in love with their nurses or doctors. It is not love at all but a dependency because you were able to help in a specific situation. Leave your ego outside and do not let it interfere with the appropriate process.

A lack of good listening has got many people and organisations into a lot of hot water. Listening does not come naturally; our ego makes sure of that. Listening is a skill and needs to be practiced.

Just because we are quiet does not mean we are listening. Far too frequently we are disinterested in the person speaking so we momentarily transport ourselves to the weekend or the coming evening's entertainment. Although it might appear we are listening, we're not paying attention, until of course the opportunity comes to launch back in so that we can get our own point across. Sometimes this is understandable, especially if you're on a course yourself and it's not stimulating in any way. Either way, your mind is going AWOL (Absent without leave!) and you need to pay attention.

When we respect the speaker and really listen to every word, it takes understanding and rapport to a deeper level. But,it is also very tiring.

I know of one CEO who made it his goal, first thing in a morning, to walk the entire shop floor and enquire as to how things were shaping up (or not as the case may be). At first no one said anything, except what they thought he wanted to hear. However, after everyone realised the walks were not just some fad, and that the CEO was genuinely interested, everyone opened up to him in a profound way. Trust had been established. This was all achieved by the CEO listening to their issues, and then following up with action. What followed was an increase in morale, trust and pride.

We've all heard the criticism, "He talks too much!" When was the last time you heard someone criticised for listening too much?

Norm Augustine, Former Chairman
LockheedMartin

It's no different on a course. The delegate should be able to be heard and feel valued for their contribution. Participation certainly needs encouraging; after all, when a delegate contributes and freely gives their own knowledge to the group, then everyone benefits.

Some people don't say much at all, but when they do it can be quite profound. This adds to the enjoyment, pleasure and interaction. Many people learn from each other; long gone are the days when all the knowledge is held by the teacher or lecturer.

It is said that half the people in the world have nothing to say but keep saying it anyway, and the other half have something to say but say nothing.

In a typical debate, people will stop listening in order to work out what they are going to say. Many times people do not talk to each other, but at each other. Watch carefully two people who are excited or passionate about a subject and watch how often they talk over each other; even their voice speed and body language will match. It's great fun to watch.

I make a real point of including everybody in a training session, even the very quite ones. Slowly but surely and with skilful questioning they will start to relax and contribute. This is a good indication that, if the quiet ones speak up, we are onto a winner.

Listen exclusively to the person speaking when they decide to contribute. Remember, 'to be interesting, be interested'. This can also give depth to your relationships, not to mention how people respect you.

Many people only have one preferred mode of communication, and can find it difficult to communicate with someone who is explaining something in a different mode (i.e. a visual person using words like picture this, how do you think this will look) compared to someone who preferred another mode, say kinaesthetic, (i.e. using words like I don't feel right with this or that doesn't hit the spot). This happened to two friends of mine who run a small business together and are very passionate about what they do. One friend was explaining something he was passionate about more in

Stop & think

Try these for size

Score
5 - Never
3 - Sometimes
1 - Always

	Never	Sometimes	Always
Do you drift off when someone goes on and on with too much detail?	☐	☐	☐
Do you prepare your next statement before the speaker has finished theirs?	☐	☐	☐
Do you listen to what only applies to you?	☐	☐	☐
Do you find yourself bringing in your own story into it before they finish?	☐	☐	☐
Do you ignore them non-verbally while pretending to listen?	☐	☐	☐
Do you find yourself interrupting the speaker regularly?	☐	☐	☐
Do you find yourself not really listening but trying to think what to say next?	☐	☐	☐
Do you find yourself looking around and not concentrating on the speaker?	☐	☐	☐

If you scored;

• 30 – 40, you are on the winning side, keep it up and examine where you could gain some extra points

• 20 – 30 most people fall between these, this can be increased identifying where you need to apply more effort.

• 15 – 19 certainly need to improve for a trainer, make a conscious effort to apply these one by one, after all it's within your interests.

• 8 – 14 poor listening skills for a trainer, can be disastrous this requires your full attention, listening is a skill and like any other skill you need to keep applying it, just an increase of 6 would make a big difference.

a visual mode and there was a huge mismatch as the kinaesthetic had difficulty connecting with him. This can happen in training try to use different techniques to cover the Visual, Auditory and Kinaesthetic delegates.

In many cases, your ability to fully focus on a conversation will depend a lot on the situation. However in training, not paying attention or focussing on what the trainer or delegate is saying is happening more than you would think.

It would be rare if you ticked all the boxes with the same comment because we respond to different circumstances in different ways. Some people are naturally excellent listeners but they are in the minority. Most people listen in different ways and utilise different sensors. When there is a formal exam or assessment at the end of a course, people will listen more intently. Conversely when there is only an informal assessment or none at all they will tend to relax and be completely different.

On one occasion my business partner and I ran a course on advanced selling techniques but we made sure the course did not end at the class room door. The delegates finished with a six week plan to implement after the course, and we followed up with them individually at the end of the six week period. In this way we ensured that the outcomes of the course were implemented and became unconsciously competent.

Chapter 4

Step 7 Story telling

"Kind words can be short and easy to speak but their echo's are truly endless"

Mother Teresa

STORY TELLING HAS existed for thousands of years as a means of sharing and exchanging information. Many ancient histories have been passed from generation to generation through the art of story telling. In training over the last few years it has become very popular to use a range of techniques to engage and inspire the group.

Today, the art of storytelling is kept alive in groups like the Scouts, where on camp the leader will sit with the group around the camp fire and tell stories about Baden Powell or some other historic scouting event. It is practiced in almost every pub every evening, and if you've been to a wedding or a funeral you will have heard many stories which all help to keep history alive.

Every experience is a potential story which can be moulded into a teaching point. The key to story telling is to match the appropriate experience with that teaching point. There are two advantages of incorporating your own experiences into training. Firstly no one can dispute the story, no matter how far fetched it might appear, and secondly if used in the proper context it will illuminate the subject and bring clarity to the point you are making.

A well told story has the benefit of drawing the delegates in, making you seem more human and grounding the subject into the real and therefore more recognisable world.

In addition to your own experiences you can make great use of other people's experiences. There are many web sites and printed books which will provide a wealth of anecdotes. It is essential for every trainer to have a systematic reading programme which should also include the print and electronic press media. Make sure you are well informed about current events.

You don't have to start with "Once upon a time..." although I once did and many people started to settle down well; within a few minutes everybody was engaged and interpreting the story in their own way.

Getting the group engaged is the name of the game. Don't over do the detail, their subconscious will make pictures, sounds, feelings, tastes and smells very quickly. To ensure the delegates keep up with you, make sure you interact with them, and let them become part of the story. It is important to include as many of the senses as possible. The people on the course actually need to feel that they are on the journey WITH YOU.

With story telling you need to take the group with you, there are hundreds of examples of stories, that will fully engage all of the delegates' senses.

Most people love to talk about themselves

With experience you will learn what stories best fit with which topics, where best to tell them in the sessions; however you must keep the goals of the curriculum in view and not stray too far, especially if you're training to a national fixed training programme.

Over the years you will learn just as much from the delegates as they will learn from you. Listen to the delegates and they will provide you will all the anecdotal material you need. However many of the examples I use come from everyday life, so be aware of what is happening around you and view everything as a possible story to be incorporated into your presentation.

It's like a comedian who is continually on the look out for new material; there is always something you can bring into your session. Before long you will have to leave some things out, and once the curriculum is in your head you can then experiment to see what sort of things go well, and achieve magical interaction to maintain maximum interest.

Here's an example: years ago, whilst discussing a particularly tedious part of the English legal system, so tedious in fact that I was struggling to focus on the topic myself, I decided to turn it into a story that got the whole group involved. What would they have done in this situation, and how would they defend themselves in court?

Another time the group was split into working groups of three and four. We watched a short film; a couple of groups were given the task of defending themselves in the role play to follow while the remainder were to prepare the case for the prosecution. Finally they all had to role play the court scene. It sounds simple, and it is, but it had a profound effect on the group.

On another occasion, a friend of mine was invited to give a short presentation to twenty or so business people on the benefits of first-aid training. She'd asked me along for support. After outlining what the course entailed and how useful it could be, she waited for some kind of response. The business people thanked her for her presentation but clearly did not pick up on the main point, which was to book themselves and colleagues on the first aid training. Instead they proceeded to move on to the next item on their agenda. With her permission I asked for a further two minutes on this important subject.

In order to make the point, I asked her to role play the part of a person who had got a peanut stuck in her throat. Luckily she was very good at this kind of thing, and as she was pretending to choke I asked the group, in a panic stricken voice, "what should I do?"

We needed to be very dramatic to draw the attention of these busy business people. The choking became more pronounced as my colleague started to simulate the start of suffocation, but still the group said very little. After a short while I asked them the following question;

"This could happen at home too. Would you know what to do?"

Without waiting for an answer I grabbed my colleague, and after some simulated (but quite realistic if I may say) abdominal thrusts to release the peanut, it only took a couple of minutes for nine of the people to sign up for that all important training.

That is the real power of story telling - relating and engaging the group so that your message really hits home, and shows them how something could affect them or their family at work and at home.

One morning I was travelling by car into a UK city for a course and I saw a collision further up the road. A car had come out of a side turn and another car, that only a few minutes earlier had overtaken me, had collided with it. Everything seemed to be in slow motion as the cars hit each other, totally writing off both cars and pushing them in to the side of the road.

Naturally I stopped to offer help, and I went over to one of the cars, which had it's driver's door and bonnet ripped off. To my utter surprise, the guy in the car was apparently fine, and there were no signs of blood or broken bones. Even the driver's suit was fully intact. Bizarrely he was smoking a cigarette whilst still sitting in the driver's seat, but the pungent odour of petrol was apparent. He told me he had rung his wife, but couldn't get through to emergency services.

What was amazing was that he said he needed the cigarette to calm him down, but he was completely unaware of the smell of petrol, and had no idea that he was seconds away from potentially blowing himself up. He was in shock, so I insisted he get out the car immediately, and as I expected within what must have been a minute the whole thing burst into flames.

Real life stories like this take you to the heart of the matter, and engage many of your senses and your imagination. You can't help but be interested in some way. Please bear in mind that you should be sensitive and not step on someone's feelings, so it's always good to introduce your stories to ensure the group have no objections. The more you can relate to the audience the better the presentation will go, and always allow the delegates to have their say, too.

> "Good humour isn't a trait of character;
> it is an art which requires practice"
>
> David Seabury

There are different types of stories for different audiences; I often use a number of examples from a truly great book - *The Magic of Metaphor* by Nick Owen.

Step 8 Keeping your audience invigorated

A S YOU CAN have a profound effect on those whom you are addressing, some of life's most profound decisions can be made during a training course or seminar. As the facilitator, you will for many years hear from people telling you how much they enjoyed your course or how much it helped to change their lives. Many a life-long friendship or business association has been forged on a training course.

I remember that at a meeting I attended, where the management had all been on a training course together, I was curious to find out who had delivered the training. So, I asked them who the trainer had been. And do you know, not one person could remember his name. All anyone could remember was his monotonous voice and that it was a man. Apparently, he had given his name and outlined what he planned to discuss, but no one remembered or could recall what was actually discussed.

In the early days of training, a fatal mistake that can lead to incredible boredom on the part of the audience was to be over dependent on your notes. Then as technology progressed, we entered the golden days of the overhead projector, and presenters became co-dependent upon overhead slides. I'm sure we all remember the presenter who got his acetates mixed up, upside down, back to front, or managed to drop them on the floor. Of course we are now firmly into the era of the audio visual aid, and still presenters are reliant on slides to help (or so they think) reinforce their messages.

Unfortunately, all this actually achieves is 'one deadly boring presenter' who does not and cannot interact with the people to whom the presentation is being made. An awful lot of time is wasted by the presenter in preparing unnecessary slides as well. Nowadays, this syndrome is frequently referred to as "Death by PowerPoint". Effectively the presenter just spends all his or her time reading exactly what is on the slide behind them, something the group are more than able to do for themselves.

This kind of presentation could be so easily improved by providing each delegate with a hard copy of the slides which could be provided beforehand for preparatory reading, or handed out afterwards as an aide memoir.

It's not necessary to have slides if you are prepared, confident and engaging. If you have to use slides keep them brief (a few key words only) so that they do not draw attention away from you as a speaker, keep them simple (plain text or clear diagrams) so that they're not a distraction, and never ever read verbatim from them. What use are you if you can't remember what's on the slides that you've created?

You have no sense of the dynamics of the group or indeed what people are thinking or feeling if you just read from slides. Presentations given in this way are flat and the presenters can be nothing but dull and boring. This just has to change now that we are in the twenty first century. In the days when courses, seminars, and assessments were held to find out what the delegate did not know, are history. Today, we assess what the delegates already know and then help them to enhance this knowledge.

- Is the glass half full or half empty?
- So what should we be doing about this?

From the day you realise that you are not interacting with the whole group you have to make one of those life changing decisions that will mean you will never be the same again. Your whole way of thinking, acting, preparing and presenting has to be transformed. You are born again and have to re-think every thing you say and do. You must make sure that you really intimately understand the subject matter. You have to prepare your material, far enough ahead, so you know, as far as possible, your whole presentation by heart. Every aspect of the presentation should be so familiar to you that you could present it in your sleep, or deliver it backwards (not that you would of course, but you might need to swap certain sections around from time to time, depending on the experience of the audience, without missing out something important).

You will find that the more you learn, the more you need to learn, so you need to keep in mind the academic or professional level that the course is designed for and who your delegates will be. With some training materials it can change regularly due to legal updates or new techniques, so to be at the stage where you are unconsciously competent you need to continually be in touch with what is going on and be researching and revising your content to ensure that it is up to date. Those trainers who do not keep abreast of changing events and techniques, and who say thing like, "I don't get paid enough to do all this research" are evidently not committed to what they are doing. What you put into a presentation is what you will get out of it, not to mention what the delegates will get.

"Encouragement is oxygen to the soul"

Anonymous

When the topic areas are mastered well, you can start to play with the 10 steps outlined in this book, like using people's names, introducing stories and accelerated learning that engages and motivates the delegate to take action long after the course has finished. No longer is it a case of, "Done that, we can forget it now".

Getting to the stage of being unconsciously competent in your presenting skills can also maintain interest and ensure high energy; you can stop worrying about delivering your course and start enjoying it. Then in turn, you can begin to spot what's going on in a group. It's like shining a torch into a dark room and seeing things a lot clearer than you did before. At this point you have the capacity to notice the small but fundamental things, the little touches that raise a good course to a great course, i.e. like the temperature of the room, or whether someone's not quite sure about a particular topic.

"Unless you try to do something beyond what you have already mastered, you will never grow"
Ralph Waldo Emerson

When you're training and you feel the mood of the room changing and the concentration of your delegates is falling, taking a moment or two of physical role play can be very beneficial. Get everyone, including you, up out of their seats and doing something - preferably connected with the course subject. You should never push people beyond their capacity to concentrate. Once people are feeling physically uncomfortable or mentally drained, they will become fidgety and you will lose them.

Many people find it very difficult to sit for hours listening to someone droning on about something they are not really interested in, so be alert for opportunities to think up techniques or exercises that can be slipped in at a moment's notice, just to keep the delegate on their toes. Also remember that some people require more regular comfort breaks than others, so build these in to the timetable for the day. An uncomfortable delegate is an absent delegate.

- Break into groups and design an action plan from this mornings work.
- Practical assessment and feedback of some sort – depending on topic content.
- Role play exercises to bring the message home.
- Group interaction through a quiz, on the topic discussed in groups.
- Memory exercise in group format.
- Use of Video and feedback

Chapter 5

Step 9 What's in a name?

"The secret of my success is a two word answer: Know people"
Harvey S. Firestone

MEMORISING SOMEONE'S NAME shows you have an interest in them. Using it can have a fantastic impact and helps to hold their interest. A lot of the time, people have name badges, but some places do not provide them, so it is worth remembering everyone's name. At the very least it looks really impressive. Name badges or not, as facilitator for the course, make a point of doing it: it can leave a lasting impression. People are flattered when they think that you consider them special enough to remember their name.

People all like to feel they are important regardless of whom the leader or the boss is. They feel that they are significant. It should be your goal to remember everyone's name within the first hour of the session. People are always looking for the acknowledgement of the leader, or perceived leader, to give them an ego boost. They want to feel that you care about them.

I attended an early breakfast business meeting with 20 people in the room. Part of the meeting was for everyone to introduce themselves and briefly outline their businesses. They were astounded when in my small piece I addressed each one by their name. This amazed most of the people in the room which resulted in a number of invitations to speak at their forthcoming

81

conferences and other events. (Read on for how this was done)

"Life literally abounds in comedy if you just look around you"
Mel Brooks

First Impressions Count

Traditionally when we first meet a new group of people (personally as well as professionally) we race round shaking everyone's hand and immediately move on the next person without any further conversation. As a result, you can't recall anyone's name. This approach is seriously flawed if you need to quickly remember everyone, because you need more information. It might not be important at a party, but if you're trying to make a good first impression, simply remembering names is vital.

Instead of just moving from one to another in a kind of chain, you might want to consider drawing a second person into a conversation you begin with the first person before you move on to concentrate on the second person. Then you can draw a third person into the conversation with the second, and so on. In this way, you have more time with each person and have the opportunity to study differences between them all. Give each person a descriptive nick name, which will help you remember.

Failure to master this will immediately mean that you will have to ask their names all over again, possibly more than once, when you address them for any other reason.

We are generally very good at recognising images, shapes, and colours that we have seen only once. It should be just as easy with a person's face, as there is so much information on offer. When you talk to or meet someone, study their face closely and try to remember what you see. Wrinkles, no wrinkles, over made up or no make up at all, jewellery or no jewellery, hair colour, skin texture, spectacles, shape of nose. Whatever you see as distinctive or could provide a mental key to help you remember is significant. It matters not what it actually is, because it's only for your information. If needs be, keep the hand shake going for that tiny bit longer (but not so long as to embarrass them) just to give you a few more seconds to let you find something to focus on.

Do they remind you of someone, or something? A friend, relative, work colleague, celebrity or politician, or animal.

82

Sometimes this connection is more useful than focussing on facial features.

The first thing that comes into your head, the initial reaction, should be the thing you focus on, and with practice you'll get quicker and the process of matching a name to the face or image you have of them gets easier. After this, say their name a few times in your head and match it up to something. I remember I met one guy called Richard, who appeared very large and solid but also very kind and gentle. Immediately there was an association with Richard the Lion heart, wearing his Royal Armour with a symbol of a lion. It worked fantastically and to this day I remember the name straight away.

When you are delivering a course, even if it's a half day course, and even if all the people are from different industries, make it your goal to memorise their names as they are introduced to you, examine them, and think about who they remind you of.

The Method

There isn't time or space in this book for me to teach you how to have a good memory – there are many other books out there that can teach you that. But very briefly, this is the kind of thing I do to try and remember names.

I remember on one occasion the course I was leading had around 15 people on it. I started by scanning the individuals as they entered the room, trying to identify who each one was reminiscent of. Luckily there was one guy who stood out so I started with him. He introduced himself as Ed Ward, and had a bald head. This was easy for me because under the lights his head almost glowed like a light bulb, which in turn reminded me of a camera's flashlight when you take a picture. So I imagined Ed taking pictures out of his head, lying in a hospital bed on a ward. I know it sounds crazy, but it's a tried and tested technique and it works.

Then there was a chap named John Dolby. He looked like a small rodent, so he had to be Little John out of the Robin Hood films, and in my mind I sat him in between two huge hi-fi speakers that incorporated Dolby noise reduction. Sometimes just by exaggerating things out of proportion can have a brilliant and memorable effect. And listening to voices can help, especially if they sound like someone you know.

To help reinforce the recall of the names, you can make up a journey in your head that relates to the people as they are positioned in the room for that course. To do this I visualise a section of a high street, with shops, banks, a bakery, hairdressers etc. I then get the name of the first delegate in the room and link that name to the start of the journey down the high street. For example, Richard the Lionheart could be protecting the bank, and then add shops or situations as you make them up along the journey. An alternative method I sometimes use is a walk round my house. Start in the bedroom, and remember a person in there. For example:

Ed takes photographs with a really old 1920's camera that makes a loud noise and gives off a puff of smoke when the picture is taken. See the flash, hear the flash and smell the smoke given off. Next go to your bathroom, and see John already in there, sat on the 'John' and listening to music with large speakers placed both sides of his head - little John Dolby. It sounds outrageous however it works beautifully, and you can add on whatever you want, working your way around the house or street and beyond.

Faces are often easier to visualise and match but you have to experiment and see what is best for you. You may find one way is best, or you might find two or more ways together make better links for you. Whatever you find, just keep experimenting and you will develop your own effective way.

An excellent book which ought to be read on the subject is '*How to develop the perfect memory*' by Dominic O'Brian.

"Many a training relationship is lost by talking at the group and assuming the level to start at"

Dan Terry

Step 10 The power of words

S IR ISAAC NEWTON, who invented shorthand, discovered that around 700 words made up two-thirds of everyday communication.

A study was carried out to see how many positive words there were compared to negative words in the English language. It was found that there were almost three negative words for every one positive word. It's little wonder people feel they can't always do things.

"Whether you think you can, or think you can't, either way you are right"

Henry Ford

The next time you hold a training session think about the power of words. After all, there are only 26 letters in the alphabet.

The daily language you and your audience use says a lot about you, e.g., do you use a proactive language filled with positive words?

Positive words/sentences	Negative words/sentences
I am *excited* to be here	I *hate* courses what time does this finish
This is a *fantastic* opportunity	I'm *confused* it said 0930am start
What a *fabulous* venue	I feel *overwhelmed* about all this
I was *over the moon* with the course	I felt *insulted* at reception
What a *brilliant* day	The toilets were *disgusting*
This *looks great* count me in	I will *dread* the rest of this day on a sales course
Better than *excellent*	I was *furious* with the last trainer/sale person/speaker
Lovely to see you all	I am *sick* of exams and assessments

You get the idea – listen out for these types of language. These can affect different people in different ways. If we are excited we tend to play down our excitement, and when we feel stressed or disappointed we tend to keep quiet about it.

We need to express our feelings and develop a language through which we can portray positive feelings. This is something we have lost in English, which is such a sterile language really.

Now, what you think, and what you feel, are two very different things:

Feeling word list (Non-Exhaustive examples only)

Words to use, words to lose

Happy	Sad	Angry	Confused	Scared	Weak	Strong
Alive	Angry	Aggravated	Anxious	Afraid	Ashamed	Active
Amused	Apathetic	Annoyed	Awkward	Anxious	Bored	Aggressive
Anxious	Awful	Burned up	Baffled	Awed	Confused	Alert
Calm	Bad	Critical	Bothered	Chicken	Defenceless	Angry
Cheerful	Blue	Disgusted	Crazy	Confused	Discouraged	Bold
Content	Crushed	Enraged	Dazed	Fearful	Embarrassed	Brave
Delighted	Depressed	Envious	Depressed	Frightened	Exhausted	Capable
Ecstatic	Disappointed	Fed up	Disorganised	Horrified	Fragile	Confident
Excited	Dissatisfied	Frustrated	Disoriented	Insecure	Frail	Determined
Fantastic	Disturbed	Furious	Distracted	Intimidated	Frustrated	Energetic
Fortune	Down	Impatient	Embarrassed	Jumpy	Guilty	Happy
Friendly	Embarrassed	Irritated	Frustrated	Lonely	Helpless	Hate
Glad	Gloomy	Mad	Helpless	Nervous	Horrible	Healthy
Good	Glum	Mean	Hopeless	Panicky (ed)	Hurtful	Intense
Great	Hate	Outraged	Lost	Shaky	Impotent	Loud
Hopeful	Hopeless	Raged	Mixed up	Shy	Inadequate	Love
Loving	Hurt	Resentful	Panicky	Stunned	Insecure	Mean
Motherly	Lonely	Sore	Paralyzed	Tense	Lifeless	Open
Optimistic	Lost		Puzzled	Terrified	Lost	Positive
Peaceful	Low		Struck	Threatened	Overwhelmed	Potent
Pleased	Miserable		Surprised	Timid	Powerless	Powerful
Proud	Pain		Trapped	Uneasy	Quiet	Quick
Relaxed	Sorry		Trouble	Unsure	Run - down	Rage
Relieved	Terrible		Uncertain	Worried	Shaky	Secure
Satisfied	Turned off		Uncomfortable		Shy	Solid
Thankful	Uneasy		Unsure		Sick	Super
Thrilled	Unhappy		Upset		Timid	Tough
Turned on	Unloved		Weak		Tired	
Up	Upset				Unsure	
Warm					Useless	
Wonderful					Vulnerable	

Try expressing your feelings as they are related to the lists above.

Watch your Language

Most people are unaware that the words they use on a regular basis help shape their world, be it good or bad, this is important in the training arena as words can have a profound effect on the group, we often become what we think about on a regular basis.

I remember a girl at school would constantly use the phrase "you are a pain in the neck" to which I never gave any further thought, what was interesting years later I remember going into a supermarket and she was serving at one of the counters with a neck collar on, I believe we become what we chronically think about.

Think about the word TRY – what a potentially awful word, there is no real commitment with this word – I will try and ring you, and I will try and get the report over to you by tomorrow, I will try and go to the gym, etc.

I remember a few years ago an avid runner friend of mine told me about his brother who had put on quite a few extra pounds and said that he wanted so desperately to lose weight and asked his brother if he could accompany him on the run as they lived close to each other, so he said to his brother I will try and be there for 6.30am and do the run before work. Do you think he turned up? No he did not, this carried on for over four days of promises. The everyday language/words that we use have a powerful effect on our everyday lives.

Say to yourself I will try and do this or that…… it doesn't have the same power as saying

I SHALL do this or do that, or I WILL give you a call at 11am.

I have had in the early days of training many delegates say to me I will try and do some revision for the end of course assessment and on many occasions they never have the time something always seems to get in the way of TRY.

When we adopt, the "words to use" in the left hand column this can go along way to working miracles for improving one's interpersonal communication during the training process. The basic idea behind this philosophy is that some words and phrases build relationships up, and some words and phrases can break relationships down as we have discovered in earlier steps. Check out Tongue Fu by Sam Horn

Since effective communication in the training field is about (in the main) using positive words to build and maintain relationships, we need to choose our words wisely. The "Words to use...Words to lose" Table above, simply facilitates a stronger, more positive emotional vocabulary.

Checkout your own daily vocabulary what words do you use on a daily basis?

And the very best of luck finding what you can do to MAKE A DIFFERENCE.

"The best effect of fine persons is felt after we have left their presence"

Ralph Waldo Emerson

Action Plans Putting things together

Please follow this action plan and solidify everything we have covered

T HIS ACTION PLAN is intended to solidify all of the steps. Some will be more challenging than others depending on your initial confidence and the opportunities you have to experiment and practice. Please remember to do one thing at a time properly and apply it. I know that you will find the results can be profound. So week by week, or even month by month depending on how often you are interacting in seminars/training etc, learn these techniques well and apply them within your everyday routine.

Action 1

Find out the delegates preferred learning style, are they predominantly a Visual, Auditory or Kinaesthetic?

1 Switch off the power point and really involve the group. How many members of a new programme can you get out to the front?

2 How long do you speak for in a typical training session/seminar?

3 Are you excellent at interacting or do you need to work on this?
Can you interact with the group?

4 Do you ever bring humour into a session – if so how and why?

Action 1 continued

Start to notice the many different types of audiences you have and what the best way to engage, motivate and inspire them is. Treat it as a competition and notice as much as you can about the group.

1 This can be achieved through exercises and observations of the group not to mention how they respond to you. For the next two weeks, concentrate your efforts in this area. I promise this will pay dividends if you are keen to make a difference.

2 Over the course of your session(s) notice how many look at you or the PowerPoint, following you with their eyes around the room.

3 Notice how many keep their head down and prefer to listen to you instead. They are usually doodling, however, they will be taking things in.

4 How many respond back to you with facial expressions, nods, muttering and generally mirroring your body language?

5 Write down what you noticed – this is important when we look back over a period of time.

6 Could you do this or was it harder than you thought?

7 What did you learn about yourself?

When I did this I realised I was a terrible listener and sometimes rushed over things. We can't see ourselves at work so we need feedback too.

Action 2

Ultimate Rapport Building Techniques

1 Start to notice how you actually build rapport with a group? What did you do?

2 What did you notice?

3 Can you now spot the different types of learning styles?

In a typical group did you spot the Visual, Auditory and Kinaesthetic and the people processing internally?

Visual - how many?

Auditory - how many?

Kinaesthetic - how many?

4 Can you adapt your presentation to fit around these different learning styles? If so how?

Action 3

It's all in the voice

1 Does your voice sound enthusiastic, loud, flat or even a little boring?

2 Try and put some passion into the topic. Even if it is a boring topic like Health and Safety, examine different ways of putting it over - more pitch, tonality etc. (Experiment with each speech). How did you get on?

3 Remember! It's Awkward at first, but, like anything you want to be good at, it just needs practice.

4 Bring in a story that you can relate to the topic. One which you have a bit of passion for. Maybe something that has happened which you felt strongly about.

   Try and get someone to tape/record yourself and then have a look at the differences between question 1 and 4.

Action 4

Using visualisation techniques

1 In this section, visualise your presentation as fantastic. All great trainers and speakers, even athletes, do this before their performance. Please try this and see how you get on.

2 Now visualise the different elements coming together. Your voice sounds great, the presentation is going great, rapport and active listening is taking place and the whole group is enjoying it.

3 Write down your experiences and date them.

By writing these down you can see/document how far you have come. How many times do you look back at old photos and things you have done only to find no information on dates etc?

Action 5

Accelerated learning

1 Can you weave in stories and create more energy?

Relate this to the visualisation you have done. Believe me, applying these techniques make for the best trainers and speakers.

2 Where are you on the energy line? Are you livelier in the morning or the afternoon?

Action 6

Two ears one mouth

1 What type of listener are you?

Where did you score on the questions with regard to listening? This is of paramount importance in training, and one area I personally have had to really work on.

2 Listen out for what is not being said?

Try and listen out for what's not said or the emotion behind what the people are saying. This helps take learning and rapport to the next level.

3 Develop some fantastic listening type questions to ensure your delegates are listening.

People hear what you are saying. However, they don't always LISTEN - sometimes people think they know what the person is going to say. Watch out for this – good listening is definitely something many of us have to work at.

Action 7

Engage with stories

1 Check out Nick Owens book the Magic of Metaphors for some excellent stories, especially if the topic requires some motivation and interaction which I believe most courses/seminars do.

Action 8

Keep your audience invigorated

1 What techniques do you use to keep your audience invigorated?

Really start to learn to think from different angles. Where training and seminars are concerned give yourself the edge – don't become the norm there are plenty of them.

 a Story telling – have you done any yet?

 b Matching and mirroring – have you tried this?

 c Using your memory - please do some of this.

2 Tap into your enthusiasm for the topic. Get excited – just go for it.

Really go for it – sometimes, to get on, you just have to do things in a different manner – you never know, you just might enjoy it.

Remember, the training course or seminar is in the delegates mind.

Action 9

What is in a name?

1 Try and remember everyones name on your next course/seminar – impossible you say: no it's NOT!

Imagine spending time developing yourself and your memory- this can have a profound effect on people.

This area pays dividends especially during a training seminar or meeting, even during networking.

This works well in conjunction with the visualisation session. I have done this hundreds of times over the years to build interest and rapport, not to mention my creditability and worth.

Remember it's like anything you do for the first time;
Awkward at first
Applying it
Automatic

Action 10

The power of words?

This fascinating area really is worth checking out. See the bibliography for further reading.

1 What words do you use on a daily basis to explain your world?

2 Start to replace each negative word, when the situation calls for it, with a positive word and I promise you, you will be amazed at the results.

Just go for it – especially in today's climate.

What sets you apart from your competition?

Remember, you can't change everyone all of the time – some people are simply not ready for this type of training. Many people do not like to interact and regardless of how hard you try they will just sit there and switch off. The number of people who do this is getting less though, as self improvement and professional development become the rule rather than the exception.

Good luck, and to find out more please visit:

www.dan-terry.co.uk.

Or, why not come along to one of my seminars.

"A closed mind is a dying mind"

Edna Ferber